W9-DGV-327

AMERICAN LEAGUE WEST

By John Clendening

THE LOS ANGELES ANGELS OF ANAHEIM, THE OAKLAND A'S, THE SEATTLE MARINERS, AND THE TEXAS RANGERS

Published in the United States of America by
The Child's World®
PO Box 326 • Chanhassen, MN 55317-0326
800-599-READ • www.childsworld.com

PHOTO CREDITS
Cover: Getty Images
Interior: AP/Wide World: 7, 8, 16, 21, 23, 31; Corbis: 9, 17, 18, 25, 26, 34, 35; Getty Images: 2, 5, 6, 10, 13, 14, 24, 27, 28, 30, 33, 37, 38, 40, 41; Robbins Photography: 15, 22.

ACKNOWLEDGMENTS
The Child's World®: Mary Berendes, Publishing Director

Manuscript and photo research by the Shoreline Publishing Group, LLC

The Design Lab: Kathleen Petelinsek, Design and Page Production

LIBRARY OF CONGRESS CATALOGING-IN-PUBLICATION DATA
Clendening, John.
American League West / by John Clendening.
p. cm. — (Behind the plate)
Includes bibliographical references and index.
ISBN-13: 978-1-59296-839-8 (library bound: alk. paper)
ISBN-10: 1-59296-839-2 (library bound: alk. paper)
1. American League of Professional Baseball Clubs—Juvenile literature. 2. Baseball teams—West (U.S.)—Juvenile literature. I. Title.
GV875.A15C44 2007
796.357'640973—dc22 2006029256

Young ace Rich Harden helped the A's win the 2006 AL West Division championship.

Contents

INTRODUCTION

Formed in 1994 when Major League Baseball changed the way its teams are organized, the AL West features some of baseball's most successful teams. The division's most recent stars have been the Los Angeles Angels of Anaheim. As the Anaheim Angels, they weren't good enough to win the AL West in 2002, finishing behind the A's. They still made the playoffs as a **wild-card** team, though—and they were good enough to win the World Series! Since that time, the Angels have won two division titles, Angel players have won an MVP and a Cy Young award, and the franchise has changed its name.

The team that has challenged the Angels the most of late is the Oakland A's, who have won nine World Series titles in their history (five of them came while the club was located in Philadelphia). In recent years, though, while the team has continued to lose top talent to other teams with higher payrolls, its ability to develop young talent has kept the A's in the hunt for the playoffs every year.

The Seattle Mariners did more than win the AL West in 2001. They won 116 games—

AMERICAN LEAGUE WEST TEAMS:

Team: Los Angeles Angels of Anaheim
Founded: 1961
Park: Angel Stadium
Park Opened: 1966
Colors: Red

Team: Oakland A's
Founded: 1901
Park: Network Associates Coliseum
Park Opened: 1966
Colors: Green and gold

Team: Seattle Mariners
Founded: 1977
Park: SAFECO Field
Park Opened: 1999
Colors: Navy blue, metallic silver, and northwest green

Team: Texas Rangers
Founded: 1961
Park: The Ballpark at Arlington
Park Opened: 1994
Colors: Red and blue

Fireworks blast and Bengie Molina leaps as the Los Angeles Angels win the 2002 World Series. They were the most recent world champs from the AL West Division.

more than any other AL team in one season in history! While the team has experienced a recent downturn since, losing three possible Hall of Famers to other teams, the addition of new young stars has renewed hope for a World Series in the Pacific Northwest.

The Texas Rangers are the only club in the AL West not to appear in the playoffs since the turn of the century. However, the team won three divisional titles between 1996 and 1999. Most recently, the Rangers are experiencing an upswing in their fortunes, and challenged both the Angels and A's for the 2004 division title up until the final week of a magical season.

A trip through the AL West reveals one team that started out in Philadelphia in 1901 and stopped in Kansas City on its way to the West Coast. Another began playing in Washington, D.C., before head-

Slugger Juan Gonzalez led the Rangers to a trio of AL West Division championships in the late 1990s.

ing to the Lone Star State. The third started out in the shadow of the Los Angeles Dodgers before moving an hour south to help secure its own identity. Believe it or not, except for a move to a new stadium, the fourth has stayed in the same place all along. The four clubs have formed the AL West ever since the league first went to three divisions in 1994. Before that, they were all part of a larger AL West.

While each of these teams has its own stories, the four teams in the AL West have two things in common: They all have endured long stretches of **futility** over their respective histories, and they all have achieved great success. In fact, today's AL West is considered one of the most competitive divisions in baseball.

Designated hitter Frank Thomas came to Oakland in 2006 and helped the A's represent the AL West in the AL Division Series.

THE LOS ANGELES ANGELS OF ANAHEIM

The Angels have been a work in progress since their founding. Under the ownership of famed Hollywood singer and actor Gene Autry, the expansion team debuted in 1961 as the Los Angeles Angels. That first season proved to be successful for the expansion Angels, who set a record that still stands for the best winning percentage by an **expansion team** in baseball history.

Former movie star and singer Gene Autry signed many big stars for his Angels team, including Reggie Jackson, shown here in 1982.

Famed actress Marilyn Monroe added a little Hollywood glamour to this 1962 Angels game, where she was joined by outfielder Albie Pearson.

Unfortunately, the team's opening act was not an indication of good things to come—at least not for a while. In 1965, the franchise changed its name to the California Angels. In 1966, as it continued to search for its own identity, the club moved out of the shadows of Dodger Stadium and the Dodgers. The new Anaheim Stadium was in largely rural Orange County, about 30 miles (48 kilometers) south of Los Angeles.

Bobby Grich, a gritty and hard-hitting second baseman, was a key part of the Angels' first division championship teams.

n 1979, Don Baylor of
the Angels led the AL in
RBI with 139, runs with
120, and clubbed a team-
high 36 homers, helping
the Angels win their first
division championship. In
most years, Baylor's stats
would have made him an easy
choice for the Most Valuable
Player. However, he played 65
games that year at designated
hitter, a position that had only
been around for six years at
he time. Some people said a
player who didn't always play
the field shouldn't be an MVP.
However, Baylor's stats
were impressive enough to
overcome this problem.
Still, through 2006, those
65 games at DH were
still the most ever by a
eague MVP.

What followed were years of **mediocrity**. The main highlight of the team's first 13 years in Anaheim was the frequent sight of pitcher Nolan Ryan in the Angels' rotation. Ryan was known as the Express, in honor of his almost unhittable fastball. He pitched four no-hitters in his eight years in an Angels' uniform from 1972 to 1979.

The club finally struck gold in 1979. Led by outfielder and designated hitter Don Baylor, the AL's Most Valuable Player (MVP), as well as future Hall of Famers Ryan and first baseman Rod Carew, the Angels won the AL West title. This would be their first-ever appearance in the playoffs. Though they lost to the Baltimore Orioles in four games, the Angels of 1979 left their mark. The theme of that year's team was "Yes We Can," a salute to the team's can-do attitude.

The magic of 1979 spurred the Angels to a run of successful seasons during the 1980s, when the team won at least 90 games four times. Featuring an exciting core of offensive stars including Carew, Baylor, Reggie Jackson, Bobby Grich, Brian Downing, Doug DeCinces, and Wally Joyner, the Angels won the AL West in 1982 and 1986, but both times was left thirsting for more when they lost the American League Championship Series (ALCS). In 1986, the Angels were one strike away from their first World Series, only to give up a home run and eventually lose to the Red Sox in seven games.

The 1990s looked like a rerun of the team's early days in Anaheim. The club never qualified for the **postseason**, coming close in 1995 but losing a one-game playoff to the Seattle Mariners after letting an 11-game lead get away.

Over the years, the Angels had become widely known as a "cursed" franchise. Not only had the team never been to the World Series, it had endured many on- and off-the-field crises. On the field, the team had seen key players such as Bobby Valentine and Mo Vaughn suffer freak injuries. Off the field, key players were killed or injured in tragic accidents. In 1992, the team bus even crashed, causing severe injuries to several passengers, including Manager Buck Rodgers. The "curse" theory was supported by the supposed fact that Anaheim Stadium had been built on an ancient American Indian burial ground.

But then came 2002. The Angels put together—

When the Angels home was built in 1966, its most famous feature was an enormous letter A beyond the centerfield fence. It was topped by a sign that let drivers on local freeways know the result of the Angels game. During a renovation in the late 1990s, the A was moved to the parking lot. Today, Angel Stadium boasts a display of fake rocks and a waterfall outside the left-centerfield fence.

Want to hear about bad luck? The Angels signed slugger Mo Vaughn for the 1992 season and paid him a big pile of money. Not known for his defense, in his first game with the Angels, Mo fell down the dugout steps chasing a foul ball. He hurt his ankle and was never really the same again. And no, he didn't make the catch.

Tim Salmon, who would retire in 2006 as the team's all-time leader in many offensive categories, had a huge year in 2002 as the Angels won their first World Series.

15

fittingly for a team that by then was owned by the Walt Disney Corporation—one of the biggest "Cinderella" seasons in baseball history. The team rebounded from a 6–14 start to win the wild-card spot in the AL playoffs. The team upset the heavily favored Yankees and then the Twins to make it to its first-ever World Series.

In the Fall Classic, the Angels defeated the Giants in seven games to win their first-ever championship. The highlight was Game 6, when

World Series hero Tim Salmon hoists the Angels' 2002 World Series championship trophy for the fans.

the Angels were trailing the Giants three games to two and entered the seventh inning behind by a score of 5–0. With only nine outs left, the team rallied to keep the series alive. Final score: Angels 6, Giants 5. The Angels went on to win Game 7 by a score of 4–1. The alleged curse was dead. And the Angels—finally—had the monkey off their backs.

In 2004 and 2005, the team won back-to-back division titles for the first time in its history, thanks in great part to the free-agent signings of superstar Vladimir Guerrero, who won the AL MVP in 2004, and ace pitcher Bartolo Colon, who won the AL Cy Young award in 2005.

Frankie "F-Rod" Rodriguez led the AL and set a team record with 47 saves in 2006.

The Angels have enjoyed unprecedented on-field success in recent years, but found controversy off it. New owner Arte Moreno, who bought the team from Disney in 2003, changed the team's name from the Anaheim Angels to the Los Angeles Angels of Anaheim in 2005. The move was argued about—and laughed at—by fans and writers around the country. However, Moreno continues to laugh last, as the Angels are routinely referred to as just the Los Angeles Angels—all while attracting the biggest crowds in their history! No matter what the team is called, today's Angels fan has never had it so good.

New Angels owner Arte Moreno, here with superstar Vladimir Guerrero, has brought new excitement and new stars to the Angels.

THE OAKLAND A'S

The official name of the Oakland A's is the Oakland Athletics. Whether based in Philadelphia, Kansas City, or Oakland, though, they've just been the A's to most baseball fans.

Connie Mack owned and managed the Athletics for more than half a century and was among the first people named to the Baseball Hall of Fame.

To appreciate the history of the Oakland A's of today, you have to go all the way back to Philadelphia in 1901, when the team was founded. Coached by legendary manager Connie Mack, the Philadelphia A's quickly became one of the most elite teams in all of baseball. They won the AL pennant in just their second season and, by 1931, had won nine AL pennants and five World Series championships.

The Philadelphia A's featured some of the greatest players in baseball history. Jimmie Foxx, the winner of the 1933 Triple Crown, was the greatest of them all. Some people called Foxx "the right-handed Babe

The powerful arms of slugging A's first baseman Jimmie Foxx put together a monster season in 1933, as he led the AL in homers, RBI, and batting average.

Ruth." There were other Hall of Famers as well, including Eddie Collins, Mickey Cochrane, and Lefty Grove—all of whom, like Foxx, won MVP honors.

The constant throughout that era was Mack, who managed the A's from 1901 all the way until 1950. That's still the longest **tenure** of any manager in baseball history. Soon after Mack was gone, the Philadelphia A's were, too . . . to Kansas City. They played there for 13 seasons without a lot of people taking notice before new owner Charlie Finley moved them to Oakland in 1968.

In Oakland, the A's donned green or gold jerseys along with gold socks and green stirrups. The team also featured a colorful cast of characters with nicknames such as Blue Moon and Catfish—and those were just the pitchers! The "Swingin' A's" of the early 1970s were the best in baseball. The team won three consecutive World Series from 1972 to 1974 behind future Hall of Famers Reggie Jackson, Catfish Hunter, and Rollie Fingers. Most colorful of all was Finley, whose experiments included using gold bases and orange baseballs—neither of which lasted long.

After their success in the early 1970s, the team went on a roller coaster ride for the next 25 years.

The A's share Network Associates Coliseum (formerly known as Oakland-Alameda County Coliseum) with the National Football League's Oakland Raiders. The arrangement first began in 1968, but the baseball team had the stadium to itself from 1982 to 1994, when the Raiders played in Los Angeles.

Catfish Hunter became a famous Hall of Fame pitcher, but he wasn't called Catfish until he joined the A's. Owner Charlie Finley wanted his players to have nicknames. He asked Jim Hunter what he liked to do. The North Carolina native said he liked to fish, so Finley said, "You're 'Catfish'!"

The A's of the early 1980s featured a type of baseball known as "Billy Ball." The manager was Billy Martin, who had once played for the Kansas City A's (and had earlier starred for the Yankees). The term described the team's talent for winning games with timely hitting, tough pitching, and even tougher defense. From 1988 to 1990, the team was back on top again. The A's went to three consecutive World Series behind the leadoff batting of Rickey Henderson, the home-run hitting "Bash Brothers" duo of Mark McGwire and Jose Canseco, and the relief pitching of Dennis Eckersley (who would be inducted into the Hall of Fame in 2004).

Of those three World Series, the 1989 Fall Classic is the most famous, or perhaps the most **infamous**. The A's were preparing to play the San Francisco Giants before Game 3 when a major earthquake shook the San Francisco Bay Area. The series, which the A's would eventually sweep, did not resume until 10 days later.

The early 1990s brought the team back down to earth. From 1993 to 1999, the A's failed to reach the postseason. By 2000, though, the A's were back on top again with one of the best young pitching staffs in baseball. Its stars included Barry

Hall of Fame relief pitcher Dennis Eckersley had one of the greatest pitching seasons ever in 1992. In his fourth straight All-Star season for the A's, "The Eck" led the AL with 51 saves and posted a tiny 1.91 ERA. Add in a 7-1 record and fewer total walks and hits allowed than innings pitched and you've got a recipe for greatness. He became one of only a handful of relievers to win the Cy Young Award as the league's top pitcher. He matched the achievement of Rollie Fingers in 1981 by also winning the league MVP award. Eckersley was inducted into the Baseball Hall of Fame in 2004.

Big Dave Stewart was an imposing mound presence; he won two games in the 1989 World Series and earned MVP honors.

A's
A's

Zito, Tim Hudson, and Mark Mulder, and the team captured the AL West championship. In 2001, the team returned to the postseason, earning a wild-card berth behind stars first baseman Jason Giambi and shortstop Miguel Tejada.

By 2002, the A's were again ready to contend for the postseason, and they did not disappoint their fans in San Francisco's East Bay. After

Lefty Barry Zito is the heart of a great A's pitching staff that has carried them to the playoffs several times.

a slow start, the A's roared into contention by the All-Star Break. Even then, though, the A's were just heating up . . . on their way to a late-season, 20-game winning streak—the longest winning streak in the history of baseball!

Despite losing several star players to other teams in recent years, the team has continued to win because of its well-regarded ability to de-

Nick Swisher is part of a new crop of talented A's hitters; he bashed 35 homers in 2006 to help the A's win the AL West.

velop young players. Recent newcomers such as shortstop and 2004 AL Rookie of the Year Bobby Crosby, slugging outfielder Nick Swisher, and closer Huston Street have become fixtures on the A's roster. In 2005, the A's started out 17-32 but finished only one game out of first place at 88-74—in the process becoming the first team in baseball history to go from 15 games under .500 to 15 games over .500 in the same season!

In 2006, the A's clinched the AL West championship behind solid efforts by Swisher, Street, and Zito and with the addition of DH Frank Thomas. The A's also finally won a division series (over the Twins) before falling to the Tigers in the ALCS.

Huston Street has become one of the AL's top closers; when A's fans see him enter the game, it usually means "game over."

THE SEATTLE MARINERS

The Seattle Mariners have packed a lot of excitement into their short history. It all started in the newly constructed Kingdome in 1977 when the new Mariners joined the AL along with the expansion Toronto Blue Jays.

The round white top of the Kingdome was home to the Mariners and a part of the Seattle skyline for more than two decades.

Early highlights were few and far between, but did include hosting the 1979 All-Star Game and future Hall of Famer Gaylord Perry winning his 300th game in 1982. Another highlight was Alvin Davis (who would later become the first member of the Mariners Hall of Fame) winning the 1984 AL Rookie of the Year Award.

Hall of Famer Gaylord Perry made the Mariners one of the many stops on his long baseball journey.

By the 1987 season, however, the Mariners were finally about to get some wind in their sails. That year marked the debut of Edgar Martinez, who would go on to become a **stalwart** in Seattle's lineup. Even better, 1987 was the year when young **phenom** Ken Griffey Jr. made his first stop in the team's minor-league system. Hope and victory were within reach.

Edgar Martinez went from being a pretty good third baseman in the late 1980s to perhaps the best designated hitter of all time.

The Mariners are the second major league baseball team to play in Seattle. The Pilots played there for only one year (1969) before moving to Milwaukee and becoming the Brewers in 1970.

The Mariners are the only team in the AL West to have played every home game in its history in the same city.

By Opening Day 1989, Griffey was in the Mariners' lineup. And he wasted no time making his mark: He hit a home run on the first pitch he ever saw at the Kingdome! From this amazing beginning, Griffey was not just a star, but *the* star, of the Mariners. Griffey is the son of Ken Griffey Sr., who himself had enjoyed a solid career in baseball. In 1990, the elder Griffey was traded to the Mariners. It was a magical moment when the Griffeys became the first father-son combination ever to play on the same team.

Also joining this new era of Mariners baseball was future star pitcher Randy Johnson, who arrived in May 1989. Opposing players found Johnson's fastball tough to hit—if not tough to see in the first place! Johnson became known as "The Big Unit," a reference not only to his height (6 feet 10 inches), but also to his place as the ace of the Mariners' staff.

Powered by their **nucleus** of young stars, the Mariners began to make waves in the AL West. By 1991, the team finished with its first-ever winning season. By 1994, yet another phenomenon—shortstop Alex Rodriguez, or "A-Rod"—had joined the team, and the Mariners were finally ready to contend for the playoffs.

At 6-10, Randy Johnson is the tallest pitcher in baseball history; he's also one of the best, overpowering opponents with size and an awesome fastball.

Then came 1995, and Mariners' history changed forever. In early August, the Mariners were 11 games behind the streaking Angels. All of a sudden, the Angels starting losing—and Seattle started winning. After an exciting finish, it all came down to a one-game playoff to determine the AL West champion. Johnson was not to be stopped. By the end of the game, The Big Unit was still on the pitcher's mound, arms raised in triumph. The team would go on to beat the New York Yankees in their first-ever playoff series, a thrilling three games to two triumph.

The 1995 season was truly a miracle. It was also a springboard to a series of successful seasons. The Mariners would win the AL West

Start the celebration! Ken Griffey Jr. slides home with the winning run in the 1995 AL Division Series, in which the Mariners upset the mighty Yankees.

again in 1997. In 2000, in their first full season playing at the all-new Safeco Field, the Mariners stayed the course, taking the AL wild-card playoff spot.

Going into 2001, however, not even the most optimistic Mariners fan could have predicted the team's level of success. That year, Seattle won more regular-season games than any other team in AL history—an incredible 116! Even more incredible is that the Mariners accomplished this feat without Griffey, Johnson, and Rodriguez. They all had left the team or had been traded. The new star in 2001 was outfielder Ichiro Suzuki, a rookie from Japan. Suzuki won the AL MVP award, the bat-

The opening of Safeco Field in 2000 signalled a new era in Mariners history; the new ballpark drew big crowds to watch an improved team.

ting title, and a Gold Glove Award for defensive excellence. Although the Yankees ended Seattle's World Series hopes that year, a new level of excellence had been set.

While the team had become used to losing star players, the one who had stayed—designated hitter Martinez—played his last game for the Mariners in 2004 after 18 years on the roster. Martinez retired after that season as the team's all-time leader in games played, runs batted in (RBIs), hits, doubles, and extra-base hits. In fact, Martinez became so successful as a DH that, upon his retirement, baseball renamed the annual designated hitter award after him!

Ichiro has clearly become the face of the franchise—and what a face his is! In 2004, on his way to the AL batting title with a .372 average, Ichiro recorded 262 hits, breaking George Sisler's 84-year-old record for most hits in a season. And when he passed 200 hits in the 2005 season, Ichiro became the first player in baseball history to reach 200 hits in each of his first five seasons. With Ichiro in a lineup that now also features sluggers Adrian Beltre and Richie Sexson, there is hope for a first World Series in the Pacific Northwest.

In 2006, the first World Baseball Classic pitted the national teams of 12 nations in a tournament to determine the world's best baseball nation. While many experts expected the Dominican Republic and the United States to dominate the competition, neither team made the final. In fact, the only player from Major League Baseball to play on the winning team was none other than Ichiro. The Japanese star led his nation's team to a surprise win over a tough team from Cuba. Outstanding pitching and great defense were the keys to Japan's win; Ichiro helped by batting .364 with 5 RBI and 4 stolen bases in eight games.

Former Japanese superstar Ichiro Suzuki has become an American superstar as well, dazzling fans and opponents with his hitting, speed, and defense.

THE TEXAS RANGERS

Many baseball fans know that President George W. Bush once owned the Texas Rangers. What some fans don't know is that the Texas Rangers got their start in the shadow of the White House. That's right—the Texas Rangers originally called Washington, D.C., home. They entered the AL as the Washington Senators in 1961. By 1972, the Senators had moved to Arlington, about halfway between Dallas and Ft. Worth, and the renamed Texas Rangers were born.

Frank Howard was a slugging star for the Washington Senators, the team that became the Texas Rangers.

While everything in Texas is supposed to be bigger, one thing that wasn't was the Rangers' original home, Turnpike Stadium, which was expanded to seat 35,694 and renamed Arlington Stadium. But everything else about the team was big right from the beginning. Its manager was legendary Hall of Famer Ted Williams, who coached the team's first season before retiring.

Then there was big slugger Frank Howard, who would homer in the first inning of the team's first game at Arlington Stadium. With that first home run, the stage was set. Watching some of the game's greatest

Baseball immortal Ted Williams briefly managed the Senators and then became the first manager of the Texas Rangers.

stars would soon become a tradition for local baseball fans. The first major star to hit the scene was Toby Harrah. In that inaugural season of 1972, he would become the first Ranger to make the AL All-Star team.

The 1974 season was truly a bonanza for the Rangers. The team went a franchise-best 86–76 and finished in second place. The Rangers featured Jeff Burroughs, the AL MVP; Mike Hargrove, the league's Rookie of the Year; and Ferguson Jenkins, the AL's Comeback Player of the Year. Not bad for one season!

Throughout the rest of the 1970s and 1980s, not many people noticed the Rangers, even though they fielded competitive teams. A major turning point, however, would come in 1989. That year, two new, key faces emerged: Bush, the new owner, and pitcher Nolan Ryan. Right from the start, Ryan was a hit. He became the first pitcher in major league history to record 5,000 career strikeouts. The following year, he would record his 300th career victory. In 1990, he would become the first pitcher to throw six career no-hitters. One year later, just when one thought Ryan couldn't top himself, he recorded his seventh and final **no-hitter** at age 44.

While the Rangers have traditionally kept blue as their primary uniform color, the team switched to red from 1994 to 1999. Uniforms featured red hats, belts, stirrup socks, and pinstripes.

Speaking of hats, Nolan Ryan entered the Hall of Fame in 1999 and was pictured on his plaque wearing a Texas Rangers cap. He is the only player whose number (34) has been retired by the team.

The Nolan Ryan Express mowed down batters like a train. Ryan set career records for most strikeouts and also pitched a record seven no-hitters.

The Rangers made sports history in 2001 when they signed superstar shortstop Alex Rodriguez to a massive contract. "A-Rod" was a free agent from Seattle and many teams pursued him, but the Rangers won the battle. They gave A-Rod a 10-year contract for—are you ready for this—$252 million! It was (and still is) the largest contract given to any player in any sport.

Shortstop Michael Young was one of the best fielders at his position before A-Rod arrived. But Young "took one for the team" and switched to second base to make room for A-Rod in the lineup. Good move by the Rangers, as Young went to win an AL batting title.

In 1994, the Rangers moved to their new home, The Ballpark at Arlington. Spurred by a new core of offensive stars, the team became one of the most feared in the league. In 1996, the Rangers were led by Ivan Rodriguez, the All-Star catcher, and outfielder Juan Gonzalez, who would be the AL MVP. The Rangers marched to their first-ever division title. They would repeat as AL West champions in 1998 and again in 1999.

In 2001, the franchise added superstar shortstop Alex Rodriguez. During his three seasons as a Ranger, A-Rod posted statistics never before thought possible for a shortstop, including an AL-best 57 homers in 2002.

After finishing in last place in each of Rodriguez's three seasons on the team, the Rangers began a new era in 2004 built around what many thought was the best young infield in baseball—powerful first baseman Mark Teixeira; multi-talented second baseman Alfonso Soriano, whom the Rangers had acquired from the Yankees in a trade for Rodriguez; shortstop Michael Young, who had previously played second base; and third baseman "Hammerin'" Hank Blalock, who had won the All-Star Game with a dramatic home run the year

Mark Teixeira has become one of the best switch-hitters of all time; in 2005, he set an all-time record for switch-hitters with 145 RBI.

before. The result was a stunning turnaround, with the team winning 89 games and battling the Angels and A's for the division crown into the last week of the season. In the process, each member of the Rangers' infield hit more than 20 home runs, only the second time in baseball history this has occurred.

The Rangers slid back to mediocrity in 2005, winning only 79 games (and Soriano moved on to the Washington Nationals). But the season was filled with offensive fireworks, which has been a staple of

"Hammerin'" Hank Blalock has anchored third base for Texas since joining the team in 2002; he's had three seasons with 90 or more RBI.

the franchise since it moved to Texas. The team hit the second most home runs (260) in baseball history, while Young won the AL batting title. As long as the Rangers continue to field powerful lineups, fans will continue to dream Texas-sized dreams for their team to make it to their first World Series.

Shortstop Michael Young hit a dramatic ninth-inning triple to give the AL the win in the 2006 All-Star Game; he was named the game's MVP.

STAT STUFF

TEAM RECORDS (THROUGH 2006)

Team	All-time Record	World Series Titles (Most Recent)	Number of Times in the Postseason	Top Manager (Wins)
Angels*	3,596–3,726	1 (2002)	5	Bill Rigney (625)
Athletics**	7,963–8,412	9 (1989)	22	Connie Mack (3,582)
Mariners	2,227–2,508	0	4	Lou Piniella (840)
Rangers***	3,416–3,889	0	3	Bobby Valentine (581)

**includes Los Angeles and California*
***includes Philadelphia and Kansas City*
****includes Washington*

AMERICAN LEAGUE WEST CAREER LEADERS (THROUGH 2006)

ANAHEIM

Category	Name (Years with Team)	Total
Batting Average	Vladimir Guerrero (2005–2006)	.328
Home Runs	Tim Salmon (1992–2004)	290
RBI	Garrett Anderson (1994–2006)	1,128
Stolen Bases	Gary Pettis (1982–87)	186
Wins	Chuck Finley (1986–1999)	165
Saves	Troy Percival (1995–2004)	316
Strikeouts	Nolan Ryan (1972–79)	2,416

AMERICAN LEAGUE WEST CAREER LEADERS (THROUGH 2006)

OAKLAND

Category	Name (Years with Team)	Total
Batting Average	Al Simmons (1924–1932, 1940–41, 1944)	.356
Home Runs	Mark McGwire (1986–1997)	363
RBI	Al Simmons (1924–1932, 1940–41, 1944)	1,178
Stolen Bases	Rickey Henderson (1979–1984, 1989–1995, 1998)	867
Wins	Eddie Plank (1901–1914)	284
Saves	Dennis Eckersley (1987–1995)	320
Strikeouts	Eddie Plank (1901–1914)	1,985

SEATTLE

Category	Name (Years with Team)	Total
Batting Average	Ichiro Suzuki (2001–2006)	.331
Home Runs	Ken Griffey Jr. (1989–1999)	398
RBI	Edgar Martinez (1987–2004)	1,261
Stolen Bases	Julio Cruz (1977–1983)	290
Wins	Jamie Moyer (1996–2006)	145
Saves	Kazuhiro Sasaki (2000–03)	129
Strikeouts	Randy Johnson (1989–1998)	2,162

MORE STAT STUFF

AMERICAN LEAGUE WEST CAREER LEADERS (THROUGH 2006)

TEXAS

Category	Name (Years with Team)	Total
Batting Average	Al Oliver (1978–1981)	.319
Home Runs	Juan Gonzalez (1989–1999, 2002–03)	372
RBI	Juan Gonzalez (1989–1999, 2002–03)	1,180
Stolen Bases	Bump Wills (1977–1981)	161
Wins	Charlie Hough (1980–1990)	139
Saves	John Wetteland (1997–2000)	150
Strikeouts	Charlie Hough (1980–1990)	1,452

GLOSSARY

expansion team—a new franchise that starts from scratch, thus increasing (or expanding) the number of clubs in a given league

futility—a repeated inability to get a given job done

infamous—well-known, but for often negative reasons

mediocrity—a steady state of poor results from an activity, in this case, poor play

no-hitter—a complete game in which the pitcher or pitchers for one team do not allow the opposing team any hits

nucleus—the central point or component around which other things are added

phenom—a young player who quickly proves to be one of the best players of any age

postseason—the playoffs, which in baseball start with the Division Series, continue with League Championship Series, and conclude with the World Series

stalwart—a person who is a steadily outstanding and dependable player for a long period of time

tenure—the amount of time a person holds a job

wild-card—a team that finishes in second place in its division but still makes the playoffs

TIMELINE

1901 The Philadelphia Athletics are founded as charter members of the AL.

1910 The Athletics win their first World Series.

1955 The Athletics move to Kansas City.

1961 The Los Angeles Angels and the Washington Senators are founded as AL expansion teams.

1966 The Angels move to Anaheim, California.

1968 The A's move to Oakland.

1972 The Washington Senators relocate to Texas and become the Rangers.

The A's win the first of three consecutive World Series.

1977 The Seattle Mariners are founded as an AL expansion team.

1979 The Angels win their first AL West title.

1989 The A's beat the San Francisco Giants in the "Bay Bridge" World Series, which is delayed by a major earthquake before Game 3.

1995 The Mariners win their first AL West title.

1996 The Rangers win their first AL West title.

2001 The Mariners set an all-time AL record for most wins in a season (116).

2002 The Angels win the World Series.

FOR MORE INFORMATION

BOOKS

Dickey, Glenn. *Champions: The Story of the First Two Oakland A's Dynasties and the Building of the Third.* Chicago: Triumph Books, 2002.

Frisch, Aaron. *The History of the Texas Rangers.* Mankato, Minn.: Creative Education, 2003.

Goodman, Michael E. *The History of the Seattle Mariners.* Mankato, Minn.: Creative Education, 2003.

Rambeck, Richard. *The History of the Anaheim Angels.* Mankato, Minn.: Creative Education, 1999.

ON THE WEB

Visit our home page for lots of links about the American League West teams: ***http://www.childsworld.com/links***

Note to Parents, Teachers, and Librarians: We routinely check our Web links to make sure they're safe, active sites—so encourage your readers to check them out!

INDEX

ABOUT THE AUTHOR

John Clendening has written about football, college basketball, and hockey for young readers. He is an award-winning former journalist who now lives and works in Texas, where he regularly attends games played by the Frisco RoughRiders, a minor league affiliate of the Texas Rangers.